STONE
WISDOM

STONE
WISDOM

Rolland G. Smith

poems and commentaries

The Kenneth G. Mills Foundation
Toronto

Library and Archives Canada Cataloguing in Publication

Smith, Rolland G., 1941-
    Stone wisdom : poems and commentaries / Rolland G. Smith ; Angela Wingfield, editor.

ISBN 978-0-919842-71-7

    I. Wingfield, Angela II. Kenneth G. Mills Foundation III. Title.

PS3569.M5385S74 2008   818'.5409   C2008-905428-8

The Kenneth G. Mills Foundation
P.O. Box 790, Station F
Toronto, Ontario M4Y 2N7, Canada
www.kgmfoundation.org
Tel: 416-410-0453 or 1-800-437-1454
Fax: 905-951-9712
Email: news@kgmfoundation.org
Visit: www.rollandgsmith.com

Cover design: Sue DiCicco
Layout design: Ellen Mann
Photography: Claude Charlebois, Rolland Smith, Ellen Mann
Illustration: Sue DiCicco

Printed in Canada

Stone Wisdom is dedicated to the memory of
Dr. Kenneth George Mills (1923-2004), whose
gifts and accomplishments can be found
and enjoyed at www.kgmfoundation.org.

And to my son Lee Rolland Smith (1968-1999),
who is forever in the hearts and minds of
those who knew him.

This is the time for all to be aware
Of the lasting power within a phrase
And to be the grace of its lasting prayer
So that the love of light is seen ablaze.

Contents

ix

Rolland Smith's poems, his gift on so many levels, rekindled in me a dormant urge to read more verse, which in his words is the "rhyme of reason." His poetry, which expands for me the already hazy defining lines of beauty, was born through the devastation of loss: the way-too-early passing of his son Lee. The tortuous agony we sometimes have to endure in life will often plant seeds of love and beauty for the next season when the pain begins to shift toward the numb. And so it came to be that seeds of poetry were sown in Rolland Smith. The agony and the ecstasy came full cycle.

I encourage you to read "Hard Words" more than once. When I do, I cry with Rolland and yet see his and then my acceptance of the Source's call.

I hope the day can come that every Second World War vet gets to read "Lest We Forget." This poem ought to be taught and perhaps memorized in any classroom during Second World War study, just as we read and memorized Walt Whitman and Civil War study. Poetry, when memorized, is appreciated on yet another level. When I finish reading a volume of Rolland's poetry, I like to select one poem and commit it to memory.

With this foreword I invite you to partake of Rolland's joy as you marvel with him in a utopia of ocean and land: Acadia. Share his worry at the loss of the stalwart ones, the trees of greatest strength and length. Accept his gifts and learn to amplify another's dream. Delve beyond the obvious and see a stone wall or an ancient hearth as you have never seen one before. Finally, leave no stone unturned. Double or triple your wonder as you feel Rolland's love for English and passion for poetry in his two former works, *Quiet Musings* and *Encore*.

Rolland defines poetry as a "link to the Divine." As I read and reread his poems, my own love of language and my wide-eyed realization of some of the content of the universe seem almost mystical. Rolland Smith's poetry, the gift that keeps on giving, is to be read and then read again as if for the very first time.

Earlier this year I returned north with the hopes of catching the daffodils and the apple blossoms in my yard. I arrived too late for the daffodils, but the privilege of peering into Rolland Smith's journal and catching his entries for April and May surely offset that loss.

Rolland's prose is part of his poetic realm of expression, and I find myself reading and rereading, not only to grasp the content but also to enjoy the English, which is as beautiful as it is original.

The content of these commentaries provokes and pushes me to ponder, for example, the tragedy and devastation that frame Myanmar; the unacceptable intolerance that is the rule of this dictatorship and that of China; and the prejudice that is still in America, hidden in some campaign rumors and innuendos and open in some declarations. Both capital punishment with its intrinsic fallibility and conspicuous consumption with its inherent arrogance are the substance of two commentaries. All of this moves us to more thinking, more motivation, and more action toward a higher level of community service.

Rolland once wrote: "Instantaneous response to need defines true service." He inspires us to respond with a loftier level of thought, motivation, and action to be of true and good service to our country, government, and fellow men and women.

Reginald J. Rinder
Lecturer: Spanish
State University of New York, New Paltz

I often watch the sun come out after a passing shower and see it ignite the lingering drops of rain clinging to twigs and trees and to the tips of bending grass. The drops either wait to evaporate to become a moisture cloud again or drop to the earth to be of service to the flora and fauna before they too return to the circle of Being. In the meantime, the sun's rays refract into a prismatic brilliance as they pass through the drops and sparkle into bursts of twinkling bright.

People are a lot like the drops of rain. We are here so briefly, clinging to something, and then one day we evaporate into the light and disappear from matter, but not from Being. Other souls, like the water drops that nurture the earth, live lives of service to humankind and they become part of what we call our history.

Both life choices are valid, for each has the sacred inner light igniting the human spirit into sparks of creative brilliance in the moment of the Now, and wonder results. For me, that wonder is words, and part of the verbal elixir is poetry. I love its discipline of meter and its surprise of rhyme and its varieties of form. Poetry has the magic of conveying a feeling that prose cannot possess. Poetry also has an innate power of passion and the ability to touch the soul through the portal of the heart.

Stone Wisdom contains selected thoughts about observing the wonder, the beauty and even the harshness of life as expressed through poetry and commentary. The commentaries were part of my professional broadcast life before I retired from daily newscasts two years ago. I still, however, follow the urge to comment on world events and everyday life via my website.

Like the drops of rain illuminated by the sun and our human choices lit by an inner light, the considerations in *Stone Wisdom* acknowledge there is more to each moment than just its passage.

It is with personal pleasure that I write the name of Ellen Mann, not only to acknowledge her profound professional editorial abilities and layout acumen, but to thank her for her consistent encouragement, many hours of gifted time, and especially for the friendship I feel every time we talk.

Special thanks go to Angela Wingfield whose editorial prowess and precise punctuation make her a grammarian with few equals.

Thank you too, Sue DiCicco, a well-known and acknowledged professional artist whose cover design added the missing grace to this project.

Thank you, Reg Rinder, for your heartfelt foreword and friendship and for sharing the love of language with your students.

COMMENTARIES

POETRY

SOME THOUGHTS ON INTEGRITY

We don't think too much about it. It's assumed to be a learned and ingrained condition of adulthood, something that we acquire as we get older, rather than something we have to work at or weigh consciously. Maybe it's time for us to remember what we learned as children, before the adult ego began its attempt to subvert the integrity of the heart. Tell the truth, don't fib, play fair, share, say you're sorry and be honorable.

It seems today that selective truth is acceptable to get what one wants or not get what one doesn't want. Bribery, lying and all forms of corporate or governmental corruption come to mind.

Integrity has a lot of brother and sister principles in its immediate family: morality, ethics, virtue, justice, prudence and even honor. The unique commonality about all of these things is that they comprise unenforceable values by which we choose to live. It's the choice that makes it tough, isn't it?

SOME THOUGHTS ON THE MEDIA

With casualties coming home from the Iraq war, we in the media need to remind ourselves about the sacred right of privacy. Some families will not want the media to intrude on their private grief. Some families will not want microphones to invade a personal solitary sadness or to hear a questioning sobbing cry that only comes when a parent must bury a child, or a wife a husband.

What we in the media need to remember in our quest to tell the story is civility, courtesy, kindness and, perhaps most of all, compassion. In the personification of suffering, the grieving have the right to keep their emotions private or to share them, as some did this week. The sharing of grief has long been acknowledged as the beginning of healing, but it is exclusively an individual choice.

There are no other rights involved. Intrusion into grief by any member of the media is not a part of the public's right to know, nor of the news media's right to find out.

Lest We Forget D-Day, Normandy, 2000

It was the day and the month the warriors returned
To the place where many died, the dawn the beaches
     burned.
The hard of then, now softened by the passage of the
     years,
It freed again the feelings that surfaced with the
     tears.

The mind and step would falter, returning to the scene.
The body now is different, the beaches now pristine.
So many came to witness the warriors return
And wondered if their courage was something they
     could learn.

Valor comes in time of need, for courage is within.
When tyranny oppresses, it rises once again.
Old warriors, we thank you, for life and limb you gave
To hold the sacred honor of the free and the brave.

You came from planes and gliders and from the ships
     at sea
And moved across the beaches to free French
     Normandy.
You now return to see the place of battle fears;
The combat dead now hold you and wipe away your
     tears.

The world now rejoices in thanks for how you fought.
It weeps for the lives that lost and too for lessons
        taught.
If there be a legacy besides long rows of white,
Let it be a world call, never the need to fight.

SOME THOUGHTS ON COURTESY

Did you see the inauguration ceremony a few weeks ago? Did you watch the State of the Union address before a joint session of Congress? Both events had audible boos from the audience. John Kerry was booed as he attended the inauguration. President Bush was booed when he mentioned his Social Security Reform agenda. Shame on those who booed. They have forgotten courtesy.

Ten years ago Raritan, New Jersey, passed a law stating that it was illegal to utter profanity in public, to be rude to a neighbor or to insult people.

In the communities of America today the elderly, the young, the weak, the poor, the ordinary, the different are often held hostage by the misdirected actions of a few who confuse rudeness with strength, insults with wit, and profanity with intellect.

Courtesy is an immutable law of the heart for it acknowledges that you and the other are one, and rudeness to one is rudeness to all, especially to oneself.

This is not something we can legislate; this is what we need to teach our children by example.

STILL LIFE

I felt the stillness of the morn
And too its graceful strength.
It passed when other thoughts were born;
'Twas sad they had some length.

The lakes and rills and flowers know
True stillness is within.
Stop and listen and they will show
How Still is genuine.

When choosing stillness evermore
First listen to your heart,
But not from where it beats its core
Or where it tears apart,

But in a beat that's deep within,
Much deeper than you know.
Go there with silence to begin
And let the stillness show.

The answer to all questions asked
Is, first let go of fear.
Let go, be still, let love unmask
The thoughts that interfere.

And when you're there as you will be
Be strong, calm and silent.
These are the traits that let you see
Love is omnipotent.

SOME THOUGHTS ON THE GLANCES OF LIFE

I trust this moment finds you in the pleasant experience of just living with joy and appreciation. We all participate in the theater of life and often worry about innocuous things and events when in fact the outcome is never the lesson; only the doing is.

This morning was one of those special days. An early morning crispness and clarity encouraged a fresh look at the meaning of life. At first, finding meaning in just a look around seems impossible, but then, if we move within the glance to the power of the imagination, meaning abounds.

The finery in the fall foliage has meaning as it ends in displays of brilliant and soothing color. Green life seems to end when the leaves go, but it sustains below the bark, and renewal is only a season away. A profound lesson for humankind if we choose to see it.

Stacked firewood for the coming cold has meaning too, for each log contains the sun's warmth and light accumulated from decades of growth. It is light energy, stored for years as the tree grew, and now it's ready to be released again as light and heat. It is stored sunlight, the same warmth folks enjoyed perhaps a hundred years ago or more.

I hope your glances are just as profound.

RIBBONS OF RED

Ribbons of red among the green—
Bright bows of life deep within
Celebrating the time between
The summer's sun and frost's season.

In fall the cold and colors roam
And then the wooded soul is free
To plan a new and greener dome.
You think that could be someday me?

The only difference is our cloak—
One is flesh and the other leaf.
What good is it to thus provoke
And hold the thinker from belief?

Some Thoughts on Connections

The appearance of whales in our bays a few days ago reminded me of the two baby gray whales that were trapped in the ice off Point Barrow, Alaska, several years ago.

Television took that story live to the world and linked people and cultures together as they watched the attempt to free the baby grays.

You may recall, to rescue the young of another species, governments put aside mistrust and sent equipment and personnel. Environmentalists and oil workers suspended their long-standing argument, to labor together for a common good, and Eskimos did everything they could to save what they normally hunt.

The two little gray whales, either by accident or design, helped us teach ourselves that the essence of life is cooperation, not competition; compassion, not conflict; and helping, to be helped.

I'll bet those whales remember.

THE CUTTING OF NEARBY TIMBER

They were not prisoners within their woods.
They lived in peaceful growth on pristine land.
Tight straight they stood in timbered
　　　neighborhoods.
To them it was their family grove and stand.

I knew them well and walked among their strength.
I watched the elders die and seedlings grow
To be the stalwart ones of greater length.
Then slaughter came. One lived—one cameo.

When saws transgressed on mountain slope's
　　　incline,
The needs of man could not yet understand
These are a sentient species and benign
Who could not stop the cut with countermand.

There is a sadness now upon this spot.
Soft tawny dust dries out the scent and loam
Where shade once cooled to stop the late day hot.
Man oft forgets the sanctity of home!

Prejudice is inherently abhorrent to the human spirit because deep down we know that the miracle of life is in its diversity, not in its created separation and fear of difference.

Prejudice, and all its aliases, particularly poverty, can disguise itself in the illusion that one is better than another. It can hide in the way we say words to describe others: *Mexican*, *Gringo*, *Jew*, *Black*, and even the non-ethnic words like *immigrant* and *foreigner* or *poor* and *disadvantaged*.

Prejudice can also manifest in rules and regulations that diminish the dignity of any society. It can harbor in actions of hatred and bigotry and sometimes in walls and fences, both real and imaginary. A comfortable commonality for all people is found in the open front yards of our hearts, not in the walled courts of intolerance—however the ego builds them or the intellect sustains them.

We must remember that prejudice grows from many seeds: statements without truth, judgments without justice, belief without compassion, and even conversation without courtesy.

WEDDING WHITE DOVES

This is the holy moment of release
Where doves in flight know their destination
And will fly, as one, to their nest of peace,
Soaring on the joy of consecration.

A ritual of heart made together,
Agreed upon before an altar light
And its force of love that knows no tether
And takes them to the vow they do recite.

"I do, I do, with all my love, I do
Take and hold, and cherish forever
The spirit's truth, and honor hereunto
Our love, no matter what, whatsoever."

Say their names, say them gently as they fly.
Their tenderness is gowned in feather white
Expressive of the light of love, whereby
Their future's bright beyond this special flight.

See freedom in the aura of your love.
Release them, this man and woman, now one,
To fly together, soaring, each as dove
Symbolic of their troth of halcyon.

Make it your lasting pledge before they fly,
To hold eternal thoughts for their embrace;
Then watch them wing and thereby sanctify
Their day, their wedding and its blessing grace.

Grant them immortal wisdom as they go,
And cast a lasting wish upon the breeze
That they may "like because" and "love although"
And honor each with courtesies that please.

Fly now, fly home, white doves of wedding bliss.
Seek your branch of peace and share currents fair,
And each of us who love you send a kiss
To hold you in the palm of future's prayer.

SOME THOUGHTS ON THE USE OF POWER

There has always been a right way and a wrong way to use power. Look at history. The wrong way was England in the seventeen hundreds, and the result was the Declaration of Independence.

When used to oppress, to control without freedom and human rights, power is a negative force and inevitably fails. When used to free the mind and the human spirit, when used to feed and shelter the hungry and the homeless, power transforms. When used to encourage, to inspire the innate divine creativity within each human being, the gentle, self-limiting side of power is actualized and the world benefits.

Intent determines whether the use of great power is positive or negative. When used for the greater good, power propels the users—governments or individuals—out of their narrow image of self-interest into an expansive awareness of benevolent responsibility.

PILE OF SHOES, AUSCHWITZ

It was a shock to see them there,
Little shoes taken in despair.
Who knew it would be a last pair
And death would be what children share?

The despicable camps of pain
That took the shoes and left in vain
The lives of many millions slain
In camps of death so inhumane.

A pile of shoes, sizes large to small,
Both new and used, some short, some tall,
With crusted dirt—the barnacle
Of trek and march and death's footfall.

All must say it: "Never again."
Let the words be not false nor feign.
Say it with truth: never again,
Never ever, never again.

SOME THOUGHTS ON THE POWER OF THOUGHT

There are some people who believe the thoughts that we have for others are seen physically in our body language and sent ethereally through an unseen energy. It's been called many things: prayer, light, vibration and even force.

Assume for a moment that our thoughts are a personal energy that we can send to someone, even to the world's leaders—the kings and princes, the dictators, presidents, premiers and prime ministers. The men and women who govern different countries are constantly being criticized or cursed by their citizens and others for one reason or another. We are all quick to criticize, but slow to praise, to encourage and even to love; thus, the leadership of the world is mostly bombarded by negative and harmful thoughts.

To help our struggling world, perhaps if we send our best thoughts to these fallible men and women, it will inspire them to seek the greater good through the medium of compromise. If it works, if a little piece of our hearts, our positive energy, our Chi can indeed be felt by these leaders, then we have everything to gain in the process. It might even encourage global agreement on contentious issues, balanced in peace and shared responsibility.

Think about it.

The sea can be both shrine and strife
Or amniotic broth of life.
Embrace her swelling crested gift
And watch the sand grains, weaving shift.
Then lunar pull and ebbing roll
Will coax a rhythm from your soul.
Your spirit then will resonate
To All That Is and meditate.

Rising, crashing, a spraying birth,
The misted salt of Mother Earth
Coats fine the face of those who stand
Astride the shore that frames the land.
It's not a sadness, not a tear,
This wetted cheek when sea is near.
It's ocean kiss and surf caress,
Anointing mind and easing stress.

There is another side to sea,
As gentle as the manatee.
It's soothing warm, a courtly flow
That moves the sand beneath the toe.
To be this sea, to be as free,
The choice is yours for you to be
Within the swells of nature's tide.
To be its grace, then stand beside.

SOME THOUGHTS ON THE MIDDLE EAST

Again the keg of powder and power has exploded into death, destruction and demands. Again through the power of vengeful choice the terrorists of the Middle East have chosen violence to aggrandize their fears and feed their hatred.

Each side condemns the other as the instigator. Each side asks its friends and neighbors and supporters around the globe to share in the accusatory finger-pointing. The peacemakers of the world, past and present, know the truth of conflict. Aggression is one thing, defense is another, and they should not be confused.

Again there are more dead: Palestinians, Lebanese, Israelis, children, fathers and mothers, all victims of hate and sometimes participants in it. How many truly believe that if we could ask the dead, "Was the hatred worth it?" we would hear an affirmation?

The instigators, wherever and whoever they may be, wish to drag all who will listen into their cocoon of fear, into their illusion of righteousness and too often into the grave.

Peace will only come when the action of mutual tolerance and the right to exist ascend to the power of forgiveness.

WAR

There comes a time, when thinking clear,
That something's changed from what we thought.
Perhaps it starts with unfound fear
And ends with imperfections caught.

But then with war and many dead
And billions spent, some say for naught,
With bodies stacked we softly tread
Upon the gift from those who fought.

Where is the sense? Our common sense
Says killing will not change the course
Of others' hate. There's no defense
When slaughter wrought has no remorse.

Now if we think that war is just
We must accept that families cry.
All sides have loss, and cry they must
When brothers, sisters, parents die.

Is there a reason for this pain
That spreads within the world's realm?
It must be more than first proclaimed
When fabrication took the helm.

If wars aren't fought for wealth or greed
With careless care for battle's knife,
Then maybe there's another need
That keeps the killing and the strife.

Do you suppose we need a way
To send our souls home to the source?
And that is why we stay the fray
And say with truth there's no recourse!

Perhaps it is an imperfection
Set deep within man's DNA;
Maybe too a soul selection
To stay in life and play the play.

Whatever's true, it's sad to hold
That we've not found another way
To live in peace and be consoled
And honor all the ways to pray.

I will tell you an ancient story of the present. Oh yes! There was light then, but it was mostly the shadow light of fear. And when the storytellers of this time told their stories, it made people afraid of life and living and unaware of the abundant choices they had at each precious moment.

The people were smothered with tales of pain and greed, of violence and victims, of worry and fear. There was little enthusiasm for life, and few claimed the abundance that was their right.

Yes, the stories of this time were told and told well, with pictures and words and sounds. They were told sometimes as they were happening, and they were often recorded to tell over and over again around the tribal fire of the tube. At the time no one realized that the constant bombardment of negative images and words without the balance of love and the continuity of context lowered the vibration of awareness and the frequency of understanding, and the interconnection of each to the other was hidden.

Instead of the gentle story greeting of "Once upon a choice," each day of stories would begin with "Good evening, everyone. Here (hear) now the news." People listened, they were informed, but they were not transformed.

Then there came a time, a moment in the now, when the collective spirit of many people spoke in a clarion voice of love. They said, "Enough! There is more to us than what you say. We are not fear; we are love and we choose it now."

And it came to pass that the storytellers of that time stopped and listened, listened to their hearts, for they were attuned to the Divine. And when they did, humanity awakened to the essence and reality of creation.

STONEHENGE

The stones of old stand tall, erect,
Forever in a mystery shroud
Of wonder where old myths select
The morning mists and hanging cloud.

I walked the rise, just up a hill,
And stepped within the circled stone.
As new day dawned, with light to spill,
I stood in silence, then alone.

The flora, fauna and the wind
Give tribute to this sacred place.
There's not a praise they would rescind
Of wordless grace they all embrace.

What rules were here within the strain
Of sacrifice and sun's new rays?
Were lives of youth, young ones in vain
Because of ceremonies' plays?

Primeval gods still speak in signs
To keep the current mind away,
For I was lost in thoughtless shrines
That held and hold me to this day.

An altar rock now fallen lays
Upon, within, the sodded lawn.
A hundred tons or more it weighs
Though lifted once by many strong.

When twice each year the solstice brings
The sunrise to a heeled point,
The apex of that stone then sings
With blessings that the gods anoint.

When at the moment of sun's rise
The rays of light are 'top this stone
And point the way, I theorize:
To something hidden, that was shone.

I know not what, but I've been there
As eons passed and stones would drift
Past wars and pain and pagan prayer
And too when Gaia's mood would shift.

So what is there for us to see
Besides a ring of standing rock?
Perhaps the circle lets us be
The ancient key that will unlock.

SOME THOUGHTS ON NATIONAL POETRY MONTH

April is National Poetry Month. Poetry is my avocation, better yet, my passion. You might rightfully ask what inspires a broadcast journalist to dwell in a poetic world. The quick answer is a balance to the daily tragedy of life. The long answer involves acknowledging the heart, spirit and nature, and the peace that comes from that awareness.

Each broadcast day contains many of the sorrowful and tragic stories of life. Emphasis is placed on information that separates our unique, yet interconnected, human nature into undesirable parts. We label them as hate, prejudice, violence, intolerance and greed.

Poetry, whether it's rap or metered verse, quatrains or sonnets, laughs or cries, clarifies and condemns and brings the intellectual and emotional senses into a radiating body of meaningful words. Poetry holds, sometimes forever, an emotion long past, a desire forgotten, a wish remembered or a splendor vanished in the illusion of time. It is also a minute connection to the elegance of verbal choice, to the beauty of form and to the emotion of words put fitly together on the palette of the mind. Poetry is both raw and sophisticated art available to the reader and listener as a subjective creation that is similar to the appreciation found in images created in oil or marble.

Some Thoughts on the Silent Gentle Folks

If you are one of them, if you are a gentle soul who never makes trouble, rarely writes letters to congressmen or to the editor or even attends town hall meetings, speaks up or denounces publicly the things you occasionally get passionate about, then listen up.

There is trouble coming, and if the gentle folk of the world don't speak up and act, then we've got bigger problems than we already have.

Where are the voices of the moderate, the gentle Muslim communities of the world over the horror and the egregious, violent attack on children at the Beslan school in Russia? Where is the condemnation of the suicide bombing of innocents? Human slaughter is not sanctioned by the Koran.

Why have not the gentle folks of this country put their voices into a collective clarion call to Washington to continue the assault weapons ban? Automatic weapons were never envisioned by our founding fathers in the constitutional right to bear arms.

It is unfortunate that sometimes only the loud, the active and the passionate minority get heard. Until the silent gentle folks rise up, until the gentle cry enough, until the gentle of the world act, our pain will continue.

THE SWING

You bid me once to swing your swing
On breezes sweet and songs they sing.
When swinging to and swinging fro,
Its gliding grace is smooth and slow.
There are smiles too as laughter brings
Remembered tones from heart-tuned strings.
A blessing on your hearth and home
As fragrance crafts aroma's tome
And brings to you love dressed in light
To bright the dark when naught is night.
For home is more than where you live.
It's flowered paths and swings active.

THE EAGLE WIND

The Aspen leaves are still. No quaking to and fro.
There's silence in the trees, the breezes do not blow.
Earth Mother's heart is sad, there are wounds upon
      her breast.
Her healing wind has gone to a peace, to a rest.

Soar, you Eagle wind, soar beyond the heart,
Take the shine that's from within and let its
      grace impart.

When all the stillness stops, the wind will reappear
To clear away the ache and dry a weeping tear.
Forever will it sing with melodies profound.
The Eagle wind's alive to sweep the higher ground.

Soar, you Eagle wind, soar beyond the heart,
Take the shine that's from within and let its
      grace impart.

The sun is saddened, though; it's lost a place to shine.
Missing are some shoulders that held a light divine.
The mountain flowers cry, for who will hug the trees?
Salvation from their sad is in the singing breeze.

Soar, you Eagle wind, soar beyond the heart,
Take the shine that's from within and let its
      grace impart.

The clouds and the valleys already miss their friend
Who soared with currents fair, playful to the end.
The lesson in the breeze, for all to hum along,
Is that the Eagle flies to sing another song.

Soar, you Eagle wind, soar beyond the heart,
Take the shine that's from within and let its
            grace impart.

Dedicated to John Denver

THE RENEWAL

How long ago was it when we did vow,
Before the sacred altar of the heart,
To share life's tests and to make it—somehow—
And hone our pledge of love long past its start?
How long ago? It doesn't seem that long,
No matter how the years have passed us by.
Perhaps it is because the union's strong,
Held by a faith that God did sanctify.
There were the blessings, all along the way,
Of seeded lives and wishes for success,
And other times when all we could, but pray
And trust the choices made would be noblesse.
We feel the love from all those gathered here.
We know the grace of friends and family near.

Some Thoughts on National Feeling

There is a tendency in time of inflicted tragedy, fearful confusion, limited information and justifiable anger to manifest the inner pain we feel as mistrust and harassment of others solely because they belong to different ethnic groups or believe something different.

Some people who live in this liberty melting pot forget that to get the pure red, white and blue of democracy you mix colors and beliefs and cultures together.

Misguided patriotism is that which accuses and condemns based solely on difference, not on fact.

Mistrust, in all its forms, is not a badge of loyalty to our country. It does not honor those who risk their lives to help others or who use their skills to solve despicable crimes. Hate and prejudice, wherever you find them, are the weapons of cowards.

Hate has never won a war. It has never solved a crime. It has never remedied an injustice. It causes them.

The Erin mist at morning side
Appending to a valley glide
Still holds a strangeness just beyond
The magic of a Celtic wand.

Ravens fly from high to low
To catch the currents' upward flow.
In swoops they call the sun to shine
Away the misted morning time.

Gray silted sheets, a ghosted cloud,
Become the valley's playful shroud,
But just above in sun's bright light
Are painted tops in lighted white.

But soon, half noon, the mist abates
And sunlight slices lacy grates
To warm the air and dry the dew
Till what is seen is color true.

Land's green then takes its rightful place—
True color of old Erin's face.
'Tis then this land becomes itself
With fairies grand and trickster elf.

I wonder, was I here before?
A feeling that I can't ignore,
For deep within is private pride
That once was there before I died.

What is it here that calls me to
Ancestral tomes, though I know few?
This land, this time, this mystic place
Is something grand I can retrace.

Perhaps it's memory in my genes,
Could be a calling, so it seems.
A spirit knowing, nothing more
That lingers o'er my body's core.

It matters not. I guess I know
That atavism will bestow
A gift that lets us all be one,
Though part of me is native son.

IRELAND

Much pain was felt before the joy
As history will attest.
Old Ireland's memory does employ
A hunger all detest.

But now the Irish share their mirth
With emerald green and mist.
'Twas not the land of "me own birth,"
But 'tis a land I've kissed.

I've come to see and be as one
With the Irish spirit.
It's there, I know; it's halcyon.
Listen and you'll hear it.

It comes from harps and leprechauns
And pipsiewaggins too.
It comes from tunes of vagabonds,
The gypsies traveling through.

I smell the peat smoke wafting past,
The green grass scented air.
Reminding me of Erin's past
And Celtic colleens fair.

The rainy mist has finally gone
And I can see the sun.
With feathers dried and birds in song
The damp is finally done.

Though fair, this day's a chilly one
Set high along the coast.
The cragged rock's today's dolmen,
Is nature's mark to toast.

But in this land forever green
The mist is part of her.
'Tis here that I have keenly seen
The sun to rain defer.

IRELAND OF MY YOUTH

I came to find the Ireland of my youth
When songs of troubled tunes and ballads sad
Were sung by family friends who knew the truth
Of dispassion's glance and famine's long bad.
Some tunes were lively songs of memories old
And others brought a tear from thoughts within
But each was sung with strength of heart and soul
As gathered guests recalled their origin.
Now here I am today on Patrick's isle
To see anew the Irish spirit bold,
And still the songs are sung in Celtic style
With tenor's pipes in singing rhythmic brogue.
The Ireland of my youth I knew from song
But here, now aged, I know where I belong.

SOME THOUGHTS ON TRAGEDY

It was terrible what happened to the Russian sub-mariners. There is probably no good way to die, unless it's being very old and comfortable in your own bed and deciding it is time for a change.

So few of us get that choice and that's why we see the violent death of others as tragedy. In most tragedies the first emotion and reaction is to blame. Usually it's directed at God. Even our insurance companies use the phrase "an act of God" when referring to cataclysmic events. Blame is a difficult assessment if you look at both the inner and the outer lessons of tragedy.

Tragedies happen so often in our world that there must be some lesson in what appears to be senseless dying. Maybe one of our missions, while we are so briefly here, is to learn how to look at what happens to us and to others, not as a random ration of pain or as bad karma or bad luck, but as a nonunderstandable participatory experience to learn compassion and even charity in a nonjudgmental venue.

If we could momentarily put aside the terrible loss of life, we'd see international cooperation where there didn't use to be any, we'd see a multinational offer to help, we'd see individuals putting their lives on the line in dangerous conditions to help save another, we'd see global empathy and collective compassion.

FIREPLACE

The fire died with a spark of
Bright and so did a piece of me
For we were alive together—
One flesh, one wood, in wars, in drought,
In famine and in sun and rain.

Insects did their infestation.
I did not know. And wood did not
Acknowledge my pain or hard hurt
When blood left my body or my
Heart ached in open deadly loss.

I did not know or care about
The sap of life that left the tree
In a woodsman's cut. When did man
Lose the connection? I suspect
The tree never did. Shame on me.

SOME THOUGHTS ON THE DEATH OF CHILDREN

The stories are too often in the news. How do you understand them?

Many years ago a New York City police officer told me about the death of his five-year-old daughter, Melissa. One night she awakened her parents and said there was a beautiful man in her room and he wanted her to go with him. Her father got up and checked the closet and under the bed to assure his daughter no one was there. This happened several times.

Once she asked her grandmother, "Who's picture is that on the wall?" "It's Jesus," her grandmother answered. Melissa said, "No, it isn't. He doesn't look like that."

The night before Melissa died, she awakened her parents three times to tell them that the beautiful man was there again. Each time her father checked the room. Each time, nothing!

Melissa's parents were devastated. But they came to believe that her short life and the beautiful man were a gift to them and all humankind. A gift of a truth. Life after life.

Every passing leaves a gift if we can see it through the pain.

LORI'S LAMENT

We cannot understand all things
But hopes are lessons from the soul
To let us know that love oft springs
Beyond the core when life was whole.

A child's smile, a fragrance fine
Or loving trills from Cardinal's call
Remind us all of what's divine
And sets the contact to enthrall.

The native mind held totems true
So spirits would become as one
But modern mind sends thoughts askew,
Not sure of this phenomenon.

Can souls return, controlling form
As tiger, eagle, cardinal too?
Of course they can and thus transform
The loss we felt when life withdrew.

It is the heart that's in the know
So let the sight now set your stage
And when the spirits choose to show,
Your knowing smile will engage.

Some Thoughts on the Shuttle Disaster

We are in an age where the extraordinary is perceived as commonplace, where the comfort of technology and science makes us feel safe in doing dangerous things, where the mastering of gravity seems routine and we expect all to go well because we've done it before. There is no routine in dying.

Death always brings routine into a tearful focus as we try to understand the why of tragedy and to find the fatal flaw of cause. While we may wonder and speculate what that is, that is not for tonight. Tonight is the time for shared grief and vicarious tears, for new heroes have fallen in the service of humankind and again they are so young.

Take time to know their names and honor them, for names are never routine, and neither is the courage that passed today.

LIGHT'S RELEASE

I see beneath the summer green
To where there's color's vibrant sheen.
There yellow's hues and carotene
Set in the leaves and in between.

Soon reddish blues will oft be seen
Within the magic of what's been.
And brilliant rays of fall's Pantene
Sit just below the green's sateen.

Another thing as I look out
To where the breeze and trees redoubt:
The forest sound is feathered soft
As zephyrs move the leaves aloft.

But when the colors brightly come
And hot noon heat is finally done,
The hard winds shake and steady blow
Till all the leaves will quake and go.

What's left is then a bristle sound
As branches slice the breeze outbound,
And weakened limbs will break and fall
As nature heeds a winter's call.

And as I pause and thus reflect
Upon our penchant to neglect,
I see some darting dancing round
The wild flowers on the ground.

It's up and down and to and fro,
No pattern where it seems to go.
It darts to left and then the right
And stalls and starts within its flight.

Why do we call it "Butterfly"
When all it does is flutter by
A blossom here, a blossom there,
Flitting, darting in the air?

With color's sight and nectar sweet
The "Butterfly" gleans pollen's treat.
Should not we change her name around
For common sense and reason sound?

But back to colors in between
The limb and twig and summer green.
If I can see leaf's color bright
Why can't I see man's aura light?

I know there's light within the soul
Where colors bright reflect the whole,
A spectrum splash of spirit's might
With waves of colors that unite.

It's truly there for I have seen
The brilliance of a smile's beam
Sent by the heart through spirit's place
To manifest as human face.

Perhaps the answer to this quest
Will come when thought is given rest.
I poke and twist and analyze
But thought appears to concretize.

With thought set loose, I then can see
The colors in the still green tree.
True too for man with thoughts' release
That lets me see a masterpiece.

In future times when children play
I'll see their eyes and will not stray.
There's color there, deep, deep within,
That comes from Source's origin.

And then I'll look at an adult,
A stranger, friend—the same result.
When fear is gone, great love appears.
Illusion's dark then disappears.

What's left is color's sound and light
Surrounding body's form and might,
And then I see perfected soul
In brilliant hues as aureole.

But now I must return to thought
And see the green and what it's brought
But I still know the truth that's in
The human soul and leaf's green skin.

SOME THOUGHTS ON FRIENDSHIP WEEK

It's coming up in a few weeks. We don't hear too much about it except from the greeting-card people, and their motivation is to sell cards and not necessarily to remind us to honor our friends.

When I was a very young man, an older person once said to me that I'd be lucky if I had more than five good friends in my lifetime. I thought that was crazy, for when you're young you have dozens of friends and buddies and pals, but as I got older I realized the truth of that statement. People, friends pass in and out of our lives.

You move, they move; divorces, career changes and transfers, and before you know it, you've lost track of your friend and haven't the slightest idea of where to find him or her.

I think it was Eleanor Roosevelt who said, "Many people walk in and out of your life, but only true friends will leave a footprint in your heart."

They do, I know. I do have five good friends in my life and for that I am grateful. I hope you do, too.

SOME THOUGHTS ON THE SAMARITAN ETHIC

A question to ponder: can we be fair to our perceived needs and to the law and at the same time embrace a Samaritan ethic to be of service to another?

There is an ongoing debate in many parts of this country on the legality of medical treatment for indigent, undocumented immigrants. Some people believe that the denial of services is rightly based on the foundation of law and there is therefore a misuse of social coffers when medical care is provided to the poor who are illegally in this country.

Belief, either in a creation theory or the evolutionary hypothesis, eventually leads to the inevitable conclusion that we are each a part of the other and all a part of All That Is. We are certainly one in the finiteness of life and in its bountiful presentation of constant choice.

The quintessential question is: what authority, what individuals have the ability or the right to detach their humanity and say to any man, woman or child who is ill, in pain, or in need, "Go. There is no help for you here"? Who could do that and still sleep comfortably?

BORDERS

Tell me when we cross the border
if you can tell five miles high.
There are no walls, no wired fence
to hold the thoughts of difference.
The earth is one as people are,
but fear holds fear within the mind.
Illusion then is concretized,
and the Oneness unrealized.

SOME THOUGHTS ON AN OLD MAN AND A DOG

I walked into a store the other day, and behind me was a guy who was telling his wife about an old man and a dog. The guy spoke openly and clearly. So I listened.

He said he had been at the vet's to get some medicine for his dog, and there on the receptionist's counter was a forlorn little dog up for adoption. The dog was small in stature, sad in look and about nine years old. Apparently the dog had been owned and loved by an 81-year-old man who was devastated that he couldn't keep the dog anymore. The old timer had to leave his apartment and move in with his son and his wife. He wanted to bring the dog, but they wouldn't let him. The little dog and the old man were heartbroken.

If there is a moral to this story, it is that sometimes adult children can't see beyond their own needs and honor the attachment that elderly parents have to things, to places, to people and to pets.

SOME THOUGHTS ON MOTHER'S DAY

We know them and call them by different names, but they all mean the same thing. *Mother, Mom, Mum,* or *Mommy,* for children, means love. The word, the name, the affection we feel just in the saying of it never changes throughout our adult life. Our mother is our first nurturer, our first caregiver, our first friend.

I honor all mothers tomorrow by remembering some of the wonderful gifts my mother gave to me, and even though she has long passed away, she lives in vibrant memory in my heart.

I remember. . .
A kiss hello and a kiss good-bye.
A hug when I hurt, even when I was an adult.
Understanding when she didn't.
Worry when she needn't.
Bragging when she shouldn't.
Giving when she couldn't.
And I will always remember her smile.

I remember, too, her happy tears and laughter and her unconditional love for me that came with every hope, every success and every failure. And in the positive memory of and love for my own mother comes an acknowledgment and an appreciation for all moms this Sunday, especially the one who made me a father.

Happy Mother's Day!

SOME THOUGHTS ON FATHER'S DAY

When I became a father, I cried. It was a little embarrassing, standing there at the nursery window, the emotion of the birth manifesting in tears of wonder and awe. I was truly surprised at my reaction. When my next child was born in the same hospital, I didn't cry, for by that time I was prepared for the overwhelming joy, fun and responsibility of being a dad.

Through the years my eyes would tear again with the delight of accomplishment and public pride as I watched my three sons grow to be men and unfold their personalities and become seekers of truths, theirs and the universe's, and then become fathers themselves.

In the dictionary the word *father* is appropriately placed between two words, *fathead* and *fathom*.

I don't know of any father who doesn't think he's been a fathead once or twice in rearing children.

Fathom, as a noun, is a measure of length, the span of two arms outstretched—the beginning of an embrace, the healing affection of a hug and one of the nicest gifts a father can receive and give, for it acknowledges the equality of appreciation of one for the other.

Two souls now blend in nuptial grace,
  beginning bliss of future's face
With hopes and wishes that endow
  as dreams embrace through wedding vow.

Be witness to their hearts within,
  both masculine and feminine,
As they begin their life anew
  to share a goal they both pursue.

If you are there where they may be,
  try helping them to always see
That tolerance is part of life,
  first for the self, then man and wife.

Rejoice in family and in friends
  for marriage starts when single ends.
This is the time for courtesy,
  conversation and prophecy.

Predict for them a noble truth
  that brings awareness to their youth:
Love is giving, a gift of heart,
  unconditional from the start.

SOME THOUGHTS ON GETTING OLD

I had the opportunity recently to spend some time with two men, one ninety and the other a hundred. Both men are pilots and still fly their own aircraft. One flies a fixed-wing aircraft and the other a gyroplane. Both are fully licensed and current in their medical certificates.

I marvel at the youthful spirit each man embraces and exemplifies, and I continue to wonder what makes some of us old at fifty and some of us young at ninety and beyond.

Health, I'm sure, has a lot to do with it, but I suspect the hidden attributes of a youthful demeanor are enthusiasm, attitude and the joy of adventure.

It was Longfellow who once wrote: "For age is an opportunity no less than youth itself, though in another dress. And as the evening twilight fades away, the sky is fitted with stars, invisible by day."

SOME THOUGHTS ON PRAYER AND LAUGHTER

There was a report a week or so ago that prayer didn't do any good in an experiment on healing. There have been other studies that suggest just the opposite. One comes from Dr. Larry Dossey, the author of *Healing Words*. He defines prayer as a benevolent concern for the well-being of another, something not necessarily attached to any dogma.

To some people a prayer is connected to a religion via a faith. To others prayer is a placebo that makes them feel a momentary good with no effect on the physical body. To those who believe they have been healed or helped by prayer, no explanation is necessary; to those who don't believe, no explanation is possible. No matter what your position, most experts agree that one should not forsake traditional medicine in the quest to be cured by alternative means.

Laughter is also a healer. Laughter may be a way to balance the disease imbalance within the body. Laughter is a conduit through which the intellect slips behind the illusion of the ego and into the knowing dimensions of awareness.

Laughing may be a gift to those who want instant access to that awareness in order to better understand and accept the experience called life.

EXERCISE

I've found a way to exercise
With joy to my old body.
A youthful trim is always wise
But age does make it shoddy.

Here's what to do if someone chides,
"Have you thought of losing weight?"
Tell them, you are and making strides
With workout sweats of late.

Just say, "I bend way over back"
And "hop into the shower."
At night I climb back in the sack
And feel the trimmer power.

I run around in circles too
And often drag my heels.
I pull out all the stops, that's true,
When exercise appeals.

In reps of three I push my luck
And jump up on the wagon.
And many times I run amuck
With stories of my braggin'.

I open up some cans of worms
And start a ball to rolling.
Many leaps of faith thus confirm
With weight there's no consoling.

When I pick up all the pieces
And I run my errands fast,
My workout time then transduces
The transfat I've amassed.

When I'm finished I am thinner
And leap in thankful praise.
Now that I'm a slimmer winner
I'm on the couch for days.

We often call ourselves a "nation of laws." What it means officially is that we collectively agree to follow specific sets of rules in order for our society to function fairly, honorably and routinely in life and through mercantile exchange.

Under this banner we do not say that all laws are perfect, absolute or immutable. What is right and just for one generation may not be so for the next, or the next, for attitudes, requirements, conditions and values change.

The founding fathers provided a framework wherein changes through the will of the people are to be made peacefully by a representative democracy, applying the art of compromise and compassion. We are the only nation on earth that has made the legal process an art form and that calls this art the practice of law.

What we might choose to do now is to simplify the understanding and the administration of law so that timely adjudication does not get bound up in a complex bureaucratic system that often requires more money than sense to get a resolution.

Bambino Curse

There once lived a team called Red Socks.
For decades their hope's on the rocks.
The Babe gave a curse
And time made it worse,
So winning a series—the block.

Then came the great play-offs O-Four.
Like Mudville they stayed on the floor,
The Yankees won three,
It looked so easy,
But Boston then evened the score.

Then finally the seventh big game
When losing would be so insane
But win it they did.
The Yankees then hid
With faces long hanging with shame.

To the series the Socks did go
Wondering if the curse would show.
Game one was then won,
The Cardinals undone
With home runs the Socks would bestow.

The other three games were supreme.
The Red Socks played great as a team,
They won in four straight
To thus punctuate
The curse of Bambino a dream.

SOME THOUGHTS ON RACE SUPREMACY

Every so often there are reports that supremacist groups are using the Internet to spread their racist message, invectives of hate, bigotry and prejudice wrapped in the darkness of anonymous cyberspace.

Just the preposterous proposition of superiority, let alone the belief that one race is better than another, belies the gift of common intellect and the inner awareness of our interconnection. The intolerant extremists who spread the festering lie of supremacy defile the truth of simple observation and investigation.

Every race has its greatness in history and culture, in the discovery of beauty through the arts, and especially in individual achievement. Race does not and cannot give its members an advantage. Race does not make one smarter or stronger; only the grace of the divine within each of us can do that, and even then it is an individual choice to embrace that gift and then be the evidence of it.

It is called *character*. Character, the essence, the heart, the spirit of a human being, is the only criterion that determines one's hierarchy.

SOME THOUGHTS ON PREJUDICE

Sometimes some of us judge others and sometimes others judge us, and often we wonder why, for we feel they didn't take time to know us. Most of us think we're pretty good people, and we are. There is, however, a tendency in our society to lump people into groups, cultures and races without taking time to know the specialness of the individual.

Let me tell you about a few individuals of science and what they did for all of us. Back in the 1800s Norbert Rillieux invented the vacuum-cup evaporation process, which revolutionized sugar refining. Lewis Latimer patented an improved carbon filament electric lamp. Andrew Beard invented the automatic coupler for railroads.

Garrett Morgan patented the automatic traffic light back in the early 1900s. Elbert Robertson designed and patented the chilled groove wheel and the third rail, both instrumental in the development of railroads.

Ernest Everett Just was an expert in cellular theory. Charles Drew developed the blood bank system, and discoveries by chemist Percy Julian helped in the treatment of glaucoma and arthritis.

These individuals worked for the good of all mankind. They all just happened to be black.

SOME THOUGHTS ON TRANSFORMATION

I saw something the other day you don't see very often. I watched a well-dressed man stop abruptly as if held by some invisible force. He was in a hurry, given his stride and determined pace, yet when he passed a public garden of blossoming roses, he suddenly stopped, put down his briefcase and turned to face the beauty that bloomed there.

There were probably sixty rosebushes, each with eight to ten blossoms festooning the prickly stems. It was a magnificent sight. The plethora of color in the softness of the morning light had stopped this busy man in his hurried quest. As he stood there surveying the garden patch and spending a moment at each bush, his gaze stopped at a particularly full bush of bright golden yellow blossoms. He reached down, not to pick but to gently touch or better yet caress this gift of nature. He kept his hand there for a long moment and once again glanced at the entire patch of extraordinary color.

I thought how fortunate I was to be reminded in such a tender private way that no matter the urgency of an appointment or how focused we are in our thoughts, when nature chooses to embrace us with her beauty, and we choose to see it, that moment transforms our thoughts into a passion, and we respond with awe.

Thank you, sir, for the reminder to take time and smell the roses.

MEDITATION

Beware the black of fear and seizure's night,
For earthly reason cannot see light's bright.
For now's the time to bide your mind and soul
As reason must swallow all illusions whole.

Now move your thoughts to where it's empty space
To thus acknowledge true the wholesome grace
Of joy and wisdom coming from the Source
Where sadness and old pain hold no remorse.

Love holds us in a brace of lasting peace
That comes to all as if it's a release
To see the life that you have chosen now
As right and just and what you did avow.

Avow you did before the council of the light
Before your spirit came into the night,
For density is hard to apprehend
When essence is about to matter blend.

Let the poets of the time tell us truth
In teaching to the learned and the youth,
For death does not diminish what I say.
It is the listening mind that does decay.

SUNDAY'S SONNET

There gathered in a room a group of souls
Intent upon the action of a choice,
Aware the intellect has cosmic holes
To swallow up the weary human voice.
Some words are said without a structured text
In hopes of a result—to then refine,
Creating new a path to see what's next;
Then hold the vision up to what's divine.
We are the songs within diversity
And harmonies in living tones of time,
But do we have a noble clarity
To hear the needed cries of the sublime?
Sustaining all our choices is the theme.
Now let us move it past a holding dream.

Some Thoughts on Educational Opportunities

I was reading an old magazine the other day in an office somewhere, and there was a story about a school board in a small town that had a policy allowing historical or religious documents to be displayed for 25 days in the school building.

The Ten Commandments was the first posting. The caveat was that no document could show disrespect to an individual, an ethnic group or a religion.

Then the school board learned that the histories of the Baha'i faith, Wicca, atheism and gay rights were to be displayed, and they quickly voted to end the posting practice.

Rather than take away the words or images and icons of various beliefs because they are controversial, rather than hide them in textbooks on dusty shelves, perhaps the school board should have considered festooning the school with as many documents as the walls could hold. And while they're at it, hanging the paintings and pictures of the great teachers from many beliefs: Moses, Mohammed, Jesus, Vishnu, Gandhi, Zoroaster, Chief Seattle, Buddha and many more.

Our children need examples of inspiration, not intolerance and fear.

Somehow we adults, as teachers, parents, neighbors and even strangers, need to increase our vigilance for signs of juvenile aberrant behavior and to speak up when we see them. More importantly, we need to be ever cognizant of the reality that we are the prime examples for our children. We set societies' criteria through our acts of kindness and through our acts of violence.

We especially need to teach our young that violence in all its forms—attack, anger, greed or jealousy—is not the adjudicator of conflict as the fantasy of cartoons and movie fiction suggests. It is the creator of conflict. It is we, as individuals, as families, as communities, who must lay down the weapons of fear, which our children emulate, and take up the powerful effective swords of principle, truth, tolerance and compassion.

The youth of today seek not only a personal and generational identity, as all young do, but deep within them, as in all, they quest for the elixir of transcendence, a feeling of creative grace that precipitates into the peace of accomplishment. The delusionary addictive adrenaline of violence cannot give anyone peace; it can only give emptiness in the spirit of being.

SOME THOUGHTS ON THE FEAR OF DIFFERENCE

A tragedy of the magnitude of 9/11 can force a tolerant democracy to become a society of contentious ideals and a collection of uncompromising ideologues. Passionate certainties are always dangerous. If we find ourselves heading that way, we might want to rethink our stand, for cemented thought always hardens into a shape that may not fit the future.

Our founding fathers demonstrated that all opinions are to be valued for their contribution to the whole and may be incorporated into the greater good, even though their singular intrinsic value may be suspect.

Shared ideals are the essence of collective growth, for they are not only the building blocks of freedom and liberty; they nurture hopes and wishes and encourage individuals to let go of demeaning ethnic profiling. When that is done, the only thing left is reason.

Despite our internal penchant for prejudice, America is still the haven for the oppressed, for the dreamer, for the builder, the scholar, the poet, the artist and the idealist, even the mystic, for all know this is the place where the manifestation of great thoughts can happen.

ANGEL IN THE MIST

There is an angel in the mist
And I know I know who it is.
I did not need to see a list
Or take a test or pass a quiz.

She's there so slight, there in the mist
I see her soul in silhouette,
Not white, but bright, more amethyst
To keep my heart as amulet.

The tiny drops of mystic rain
Define her image and her grace.
Her music soars with each refrain
As I embrace her wings of lace.

The angel part of each of us
Is known within and thus without,
Each spirit's heart harmonious
To all our gifts, denying doubt.

Old dusted thoughts, still mine somehow,
Now fill my full and mirrored mind.
I loved her then and love her now,
This angel of the mist refined.

NATURE'S SONNET

It's the softness of life that will focus
The mind into the acceptance of loss.
Some see nature as a hocus-pocus,
Fearing not our detritus albatross.
'Tis true we are the nature we abuse,
And our separation seeks no suture.
We pollute and destroy with no excuse.
The present sees no need for the future.
There will come a time of reparation
When balance loses its sentient weight,
And man will realize his causation,
Though it may then be too late to abate.
See your connection to the spirit whole
And know what we befoul must be our soul.

SOME THOUGHTS ON THE IMAGES OF WAR

For its own reasons, probably more political than out of concern for family grief, the Bush administration for the last several months has not allowed any pictures of American coffins returning from Iraq to be broadcast or printed. Not until recent pictures appeared on the Internet.

Granted it is a negative message that images of flag-draped coffins send home, and that's why all administrations involved in war have kept images of this kind as quiet as possible.

In Vietnam I've covered the war and the coffins coming home. I've seen the dead in Croatia and I've reported the mortality count in numerous wars and conflicts since the sixties.

What governments have always failed to acknowledge is that once a warrior is dead, politics end. The dignity of name is important to the validity of service, not only to the family, but to the social and patriotic permanence of our society. Heroes are honored, not hidden.

Hang the politics—these are our dead. They served by choice and honor. They died by circumstance and the hatred of another. Let us acknowledge their remains with images and names and bugle calls in public.

BLESSINGS LOST

What if we named all blessings thought
But lost the ones that we forgot?
Would then we see the list we lost
As precious gifts again besought?

And what if, too, we loved each soul
And saw ourselves in them unfold?
Would then indifference change to love?
Would thoughts be guided from above?

Lofty thoughts can oft inspire
To be the peace of soul's desire.
Thoughts have their strength when seasoned pure,
Attached to Source that does allure.

If thanks is said for all we know,
Forgetting naught, would then it show
Abundance is not things but grace
Of substance shared that all embrace?

We know of those who need much more
And cannot pay for pills and cure
And must have help with basic need
But some of us embrace a greed.

Not me, you say, and I say too
But of the many we are few.
And then I looked at what I gave,
A shame I'll hide unto the grave.

Some Thoughts on Global Warming

Despite the fact that some individuals and organizations are trying to convince us otherwise, there is scientific evidence showing that human influence has contributed substantially to global warming and that the earth will get a lot hotter than previously predicted. Grape growers in Spain are worried. Islanders in the South Pacific are worried. We ought to be worried.

What global warming means for our children's children is beyond devastating. Possibly the melting of the polar ice caps, thereby raising the oceans' levels, flooding low-lying areas like Florida, Holland and much of the world's coastlines. Very troubling possibilities. Crop failures, dust bowls, species extinction. Look at the latest UN website, www.un.org/works; it's a good website and filled with global-warming reports and other environmental information for serious consideration.

Nearly forty years ago satellite and space technologies gave us a view of our planet never before seen by humankind. From deep in space we saw a shimmering globe without borders, without boundaries, without fences and walls. We began to see a whole living system, with all life interrelated and interdependent. We saw the effect of choice becoming the affect of life.

What can we do? No longer can the individual look only to the corporate polluter and say there is the source of our pain. It's part of it, but until we as individuals no longer tolerate pollution and pollutants in ourselves and in our work environments, and let our voices be heard in a clarion call to stop, we will continue to befoul our nest for future generations.

We forget that we are the nature we abuse, and if we don't protect our environment, extinction will.

GIFTS

To be a gift in this fast age,
Hold steady to your thought sincere,
As empathetic passerby,
Enthusing all to persevere.

Some say a silent mind-refrain,
"Let's Am my I and be I am
To take my thoughts past ethnic fear
And change my ego wolf to lamb."

This is a truth and this I know:
Within each soul there is a gift.
The proof is there within your own.
See it, be it and feel the shift.

Once you know it within your heart
You cannot loose it from your mind.
Gifts manifest in every form
As harlot, artist, all mankind.

Who is a gift each moment cast?
It's you, it's him, it's her, it's me,
It's Source within, a piece of light
That resonates for all to see.

To be a gift you need not be
Attached to icons celestial.
Just place your heart within the Light
And amplify another's dream.

Co-anchoring the CBS
morning program in 1987

Interviewing the Dalai Lama

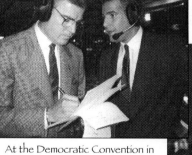

At the Democratic Convention in
New York City, 1992

Receiving one of
eleven Emmy awards

At the GOP (Republican) Convention in New York City, 2004

With Pope John Paul II in Rome

With Frank Sinatra at an event at the Friars Club in New York City

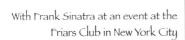

On a United Nations panel in the 1970s

Hosting a town hall meeting with
presidential candidate Bill Clinton

At the White House with
President George H. W. Bush

At Mount St. Helens just after it
erupted in 1980

With my friend John Denver

At Stonehenge in 2007

Skiing in Aspen

At home in the Hudson Valley

SOME THOUGHTS ON "NO PROBLEM"

It happened the other day to a friend of mine. It was unusual enough for him to comment on it. He's a professor at a college so his contact with young people is extensive. My friend had his arms full of papers and books, and a young student held the door for him. The professor said, "Thank you," and the response he got was, "You're welcome." The professor was surprised since most times he gets the response of "No problem."

"You're welcome" are the words most of us older folks were taught to say to "Thank you." Today's young people usually respond with "No problem." I don't know where that comes from, but "No problem" is not the etiquette response to "Thank you." If anything, it's a euphemism for "You're welcome."

I acknowledge that language changes. New words and phrases get added to acceptable usage every year, but part of everyday life is the standard of courtesy. Old-fashioned thinking, perhaps. But that's me.

You know what I'm saying, dude?

Some Thoughts on Ice Cream

We've all had some at one time or another, and since it's summer and it's gonna be hot this weekend, why not some thoughts on it.

Let's take vanilla. The natural version gets its flavor from the bean of a tropical orchid. And the artificial version gets its flavor from the treatment of wood pulp with sulfuric acid. Some manufacturers use the real stuff and others use the wood pulp. It's a matter of cost.

Ice cream is apparently an American concoction dating back to colonial times, but it wasn't produced commercially until 1851.

Much of our ice cream is a frozen mishmash of simple chemistry and government regulations. The rules ensure that your ice cream is not more than 50 percent air and that it contains milk fat.

Ice cream sales soar in the summer months, but it should be the other way around. Ice cream is loaded with calories, a unit of measurement of potential heat. You may think ice cream cools you down, but in fact, the effect is to make you hotter. Go figure.

WAITING TABLES

Tabled company, most unknown,
Furtive glances, exchanged or sown.
Aroma binds and flavor holds
The thoughts of strangers in the folds
Of mindless space and clinking glass.
Enough of that. She's here at last.

HAIKU

She left, I was cold.
The light of spirit has warmth.
Presence radiates.

SOME THOUGHTS ON LUNCH

I sat at a mall lunch table recently and watched the passersby. There were young mothers and their babies in strollers, usually two by two. There were old folks with canes who kept to the aisle sides for they walked more slowly than the rest. There were several groups of youngsters, boys and girls together, most in their early teens and others a little older, but they all walked and looked and shopped in packs like wolves, all the while playing, running and teasing one another.

The energy of the little walkers was wonderful to watch: little ones, the toddlers to the seven-year-olds; those who wanted to walk or were a little too old for the stroller. Their energy was astounding and infectious. One little girl not only kept up with her fast-paced mother but twirled and leaped and danced as she kept stride.

I'd forgotten how educational it is to watch people. If you watch long enough, you see yourself at every age you can remember and at every age you'll ever be if you live long enough.

If you ever need an example of oneness and our interconnectedness, go to a mall. Just sit and watch.

WHERE IS "AWAY"?

I've wondered now for quite a while
Where is this place we call "away"?
It must be big and vastly vile
Just like the hell from old Dante.

Each day the world takes its trash
That no one wants and lets it go.
There's paper, cans and blackened ash
With so much tonnage tossed heave-ho.

Immense the piles of useless stuff
In bins and carts and plastic bags.
You'd think we have more than enough,
But then we toss good clothes as rags.

Someday there may be no more space
To put the stuff we throw away.
What then of us, the Human Race?
Do we get tossed as our doomsday?

SOME THOUGHTS ON THE WHYS OF LIFE

We often get answers to the questions of who and what and where and when, but the whys are a little harder to come by.

For instance, why is it that after the tragedy of Nixmary Brown so many people have come forward to report child-abuse cases? A phenomenal increase last week alone, and a number of children removed from abusive households.

Why is it that it takes the death of firefighters before the department issues personal ropes as standard firefighting equipment?

Why is that it takes the death of several miners before the government promises new safety rules and the better use of technology?

Why is it that it takes the death of several police officers before the department changes from six-bullet revolvers to nine-shot automatics?

Why is it that it takes the death of pedestrians before a speed limit is lowered or a traffic light is put in place?

Are we not aware of need or danger or abuse before death brings it out? Why is it that dying must always be the catalyst of change?

CHIMNEY SLEEP

The wind blows free where once a hearth held fire.
Blackened stones mark the passive want for more
Of what was once the warmth of heart's desire,
Where in the flames of hope new dreams would soar.
Alone, it stands as cenotaph to man,
Whose hands and heart set crafted shape in stone.
But now its task is new—custodian
To the timbers fallen—no more a home.
The sentient stones remember family smiles
When tickled by the prairie wind that slides
And glides o'er cemented stones and beguiles
All those who know the joy of firesides.
Stand before the ancient hearth. Close your eyes.
A flavor of the past will oft surprise.

© Charlebois Photography

Some Thoughts on the State of the Union

It is the annual responsibility of the President of the United States to tell Congress and subsequently the citizenry what shape we're in. Traditionally these speeches are part wish list, part cheerleading, part hope, and all political.

There was perhaps one exception to the modern-day political addresses. It came in January of 1941. Franklin Roosevelt was President, and in his message to Congress he formulated his now-famous four freedoms. They are powerful enough to still be sacred today. Roosevelt identified them as freedom of speech and expression, freedom of every person to worship God in his own way, freedom from want, and freedom from fear.

Today in this eclectic political environment we need more inspiration and less manipulation. We have become a nation of dangerously passionate certainties.

Those who choose a life of service through the political process should remind themselves daily of their responsibility. But divide the word into two: *response* and *ability*. And then be the evidence of it.

I would hope in this new century of elected representatives that they would never underestimate the intelligence of their constituency, that they would elucidate more than advocate and that they would retain the courage of doubt, as well as conviction.

SOME THOUGHTS ON APPEARANCES

In these terrorist times, I acknowledge the difficulty of the U.S. Border Patrol and appreciate the good job they are doing, but if there is one area of deficiency, it is in courtesy, the common variety.

Returning from Canada this week, we approached the border crossing with the car window rolled down; we smiled and said, "Good afternoon!" as we handed an agent our passports. No response from the agent.

"Anything to declare?" he said abruptly.

"Nothing," we answered, and he waved us on.

Returning to the United States, even if I've only been gone for a few days, always generates in me a feeling of pride. This is a special country. We are known for our generosity, our compassion for just causes, and our guaranteed freedoms and equal opportunity.

Granted, the agent we encountered may have had a bad day, we all do from time to time, but for citizens returning home and for visitors to our country, I think the courtesy of a pleasant greeting should be the first thing one receives. The greater the country the bigger its courtesy ought to be.

ELECTION LIMERICK

Some thinking today on the pain
of this past election campaign—
        a rhyming viewpoint
        to scold, not anoint.
How negative drives us insane!

Notice it's easier to breathe
with no more political sleaze.
        The ads are all gone.
        Let's vow from here on
to demand politics that please.

Imagine what that would be like
back to times of Stassen and Ike.
        All words must be clean,
        no phrase could be mean,
commercials could only unite.

Start it with political speech,
and the rule to follow for each:
        find something that's nice,
        that's true and precise
with phrases that honor and teach.

Maybe we should make it a law
for parties to lead or withdraw.
        All ads must be true—
        now that would be new—
all perfect, no lies, not a flaw.

Tell us truthfully where you stand.
If you need it, bring in a band.
        Keep it clear! direct!
        the truth in effect,
and politics would then be grand.

© Charlebois Photography

Some Thoughts on Rumor and Innuendo

Even since the Democrats' presidential race came down to two candidates, rumors and innuendo have run rampant over the Internet. I've received dozens of blatantly false e-mails purporting to be true in order to discredit, smear and malign the candidate. The false accusations have attacked both Barrack Obama and Hillary Clinton.

What is disappointing to me is that many people forward these pieces of junk to their litany of e-mail friends without checking the facts and without any thought of the harm they are doing and the false witness they are spreading.

I won't repeat the allegations because even if there were a shred of truth in them, some investigative reporter would have checked it out long ago. Rumor and innuendo, however they are spread, always belie the truth with a fetid falsity of illusion's fiction.

Back during the Franklin Roosevelt administration some of his opponents spread rumors that his Democrats had plundered the gold in Fort Knox to pull the country out of the Depression.

In 1953, President Dwight Eisenhower was pressured to have the gold counted. When the last bar was tabulated, it was short of what was supposed to be there. Ten dollars short.

Just to even up the books, Mrs. Georgia Clark, the longtime treasurer of the United States, sent the government a personal check for ten dollars to cover the missing funds.

The rumor went away. In this time of resurging election rhetoric how many more rumors would go away if all of us did more checking and less gossiping?

I've become a liberal again because of rude intolerance. It was once again the action of a political regimen. I'll probably change again and again, for each side too often embraces actions that are not in the grandest vision of themselves or their founding principles.

It wasn't hard for me to change. I've done it before and will do it again. Back and forth I get frustrated by the intent of rude action. The change to liberal didn't hurt, and I still feel like I'm the same person, but discourtesies always push me off the neutral fence where I usually like to stay.

I sit on top of that electoral fence, watching the ebb and flow of American political pathology. Recently I empirically experienced the evangelical side of political pursuit. I watched as it embraced and even held and almost imprisoned the constitutionally guaranteed freedoms of thought, religion, speech and much of the press. It lumped all of those nonsectarian guarantees into a fictitious amendment of the religious right that guarantees those rights only to those who believe in the absoluteness of the Holy Bible.

Dogmatic passion should never create a political position. The brilliance of the need for separation of church and state by our founding fathers sustains its sacred need even to modern times.

I'll leave the efficacy of the Bible to scholars, but discourtesy, dispassion and intolerance are a reasonable target for judgment, especially when conceived and performed in a public display. It says to me: conservatives no longer embrace the compassion of understanding; no longer do they elegantly argue for restraint and limits; and no longer do they embrace the long-held tenet that "Less is more," for they are blinded by the elusive dogma of belief, no matter the denomination.

It always seems to take a catastrophic event to remind us of just how interconnected we are. A couple of small transmission lines in northern Ohio malfunction for some reason, and hundreds of millions of people lose power, experiencing all the inconvenience that that entails.

A traveler gets a virus in Hong Kong, and hundreds of people get ill half a world away. A rumor rumbles on Wall Street, and world markets are sent tumbling and trembling.

Perhaps, every so often we need these kinds of connecting reminders, for our tendency is to see ourselves, our needs and our lives as singular rather than interactively collective and reflective. It truly is an illusion that life is singular. Life's successes, individual well-being, and community stability are always tied to others. We designed our mechanical systems that way even if we have forgotten it.

Perhaps the lesson here, if we choose to see it, is that if one succeeds, then so do all, and if one fails, we all do in some way.

ARCTICONDA COLD

The warmth of a long-ago sun spreads into my room as a log fire burns its way to ash, giving back the heat and light of many seasons' growth. Fluid flames dance in a flickering grace of form and orange light. Heat is the result, light a soft by-product.

A few feet away is the cold. It is a stinging cold with only a window glass to hold it back. The window is double glass, a bulwark of silica that another temperature and time turned into a transparent glazing of clarity and protection.

In old houses with single panes of flawed glass, frost would decorate the panes into a translucent crystal of art, but not now. Modern houses are too tight for nature's cryogenic beauty to seep in and paint the panes with a cameo of cold. Too bad! How many kids today will miss the vision of feathered frost on the inside of a window-pane where they can scratch their own design into the sheet of condensed ice.

Just beyond my outer pane is an astringent cold that if you stepped outside without protection, would burn with negative degrees, blister the skin, blink the eyes to tears and tighten the inner nose when breath is necessary. It's an arctic tight. Not a tight of clothes and layers, but a tightness of breath. It's like an invisible contorting serpent, a tightening arctic snake that strikes with every breath. Its tightness smothers and suffocates in a vapor of ever-constricting cold.

But I'm inside and warm and I feel safe. Proximity to potential danger seems to do that. Other dangers will evoke a similar feeling. High winds, floods, blizzards, extreme cold and even summer heat can harm, but if we feel safe, protected while near the danger, then the rest of the feeling and fear basks in the comfort of illusion. Safety is only as good as the protection that holds back the danger.

The glass in the window keeps me feeling safe and sustains my sense of comfort. The cold on the other side sets a tension for possible attack but cannot penetrate the timid barrier of wood and window. It is the knowing fierceness of potential danger that keeps me in the fort of comfort.

Damn, it's cold outside!

FIRE BEAR

I see the aura of your heart, Great Bear—
A light reflecting from your Arctic soul,
A bright and holy flame, a Croix de Guerre
Of light, from ancient battles you extol.

Teach us, Great Bear, from frigid strength of cold,
That power is within despite the cloak
Of fur or skin or auguries foretold.
Guard your sacred light—man will not provoke.

© iStockphoto.com/John Pitcher

SOME THOUGHTS ON SECURITY

I was in Philadelphia recently and decided to see the Liberty Bell. It's one of our national treasures that I'd not seen before.

It was a nice day. Small crowds, families mostly and a few foreign visitors. There were two security agencies manning the entrance to the Liberty Bell: the National Park Service security with weapons and the Homeland Security folks with weapons.

Everyone had to go through the scanner checkpoints. Little kids, seven- to eight-year-olds, in front of me were gruffly told to empty their pockets and take off their caps and their sweatshirts tied around their waists.

I had to remove my watch, change and stuff in my pockets and my belt. I went through fine, and the security guy said, "Do you have a wallet?" "Yes," I answered. "Go back and put it through," he said.

I'm all for security—security with common sense. Somehow my visit to the Liberty Bell lost its mystique and a lot of its symbolism. The liberty that once resonated with the ringing of the bell vanished with the scanner, the weapons and the attitude of the security personnel.

Some Thoughts on Contention

Look at the reality television shows today masquerading as redeeming entertainment. Watch the violent talk shows; listen to the argumentative broadcast pundits. Read the headlines; look at the covers of the national news magazines. Most of what we see and read is based on contention, conflict and conquest.

Perhaps we have become a society of contentious citizens, of noncompromising ideologues, a land of absolutists. If so, we might want to rethink our stand, for cemented thought always hardens into a shape that may not fit the future. Our founding fathers demonstrated that noble ideals and practical principles are to be incorporated into the rule of law with compromise and even compassion and valued for their contribution to the whole, even though their singular intrinsic value may be less than desired.

Shared ideals are the essence of collective growth, for not only are they the building blocks of freedom, but also they nurture hopes and wishes and encourage individuals to let go of demeaning selfish evaluations and dangerously passionate certainties. When that is done, the two things left are reason and common sense. With them comes the understanding that grace and elegance are the only ingredients that can raise us individually and collectively to the realm of greatness. I suspect the choice is easier than we think; we just have to remember that it is.

SOME THOUGHTS ON FRIGHT

I suppose everybody is frightened by something sometime. We have all sorts of phobias documented by science that give legitimacy to our fears: acrophobia, tristadecaphobia, hydrophobia and so on. *Phobia* is a Greek word meaning "fear."

After 9/11, and rightfully so, many of us developed terrorphobia. We are worried that some misfits who have no concept of the real world will again kill indiscriminately in order to effect fear and punishment.

In many ways these terrorists are a lot like the road-rage guys. It's their way or no way. The road "rager" will dart dangerously in and out of traffic, creating fear and anger and counter-rage.

This is where we have to be careful. If we let our counter-rage, our anger, or the fear encouraged by government comment or actions to control our common sense, then we give up our franchise of choice and many of the freedoms that come with that franchise.

President Roosevelt was right when he said, "The only thing we have to fear is fear itself." I think we've forgotten it lately.

SOME THOUGHTS ON THE STEALTH

What is it about the stealth airplane that intrigues and tantalizes the adult mind into childlike wonder? I was about to find out. I was excited. Since I am a general aviation pilot, I did want to see this still super-secret stealth up close! But not too close. Secrets, you know.

The place was an air show in arid southern New Mexico: Alamogordo. Even the name sounds ominous. It's hot, remote and surrounded by secrets. The first atom bomb was tested at nearby White Sands. Alamogordo: the home of Holloman Air Force Base, the Forty-ninth Fighter Wing and the F-117 Nighthawk stealth fighter.

I was going to have a face-to-face meeting with the mythical angular composite dragon and with the men who knew and flew the beast. I'd never seen the stealth F-117 fighter or the B-2 Spirit bomber in person before. My previous experience and exposure to stealth technology had been still pictures, sanitized distant video and scientific words that painted more of a myth than an explanation. Secrets again.

It was air show day at Holloman. As I walked across the tarmac, already preheating in the morning sun, I felt apprehensive. There were many familiar things around to ease my tension, but my mind ignored the familiarity. This was a place of dichotomies. The past, present and experimental airplanes existed all in one place: biplanes, propeller aircraft, military and civilian, old jets and new. I walked the maze to center field.

Then, there they were! Two black geometrics looking like gargantuan black wasps dangling their spindly legs. They were a riveted collection of ebony triangles and trapezoids, corralled by a double barrier of ceremonial crimson ropes. A four-foot No Admittance zone existed between the elegant rows of velvet red.

Behind the second rope, almost at attention, armed guards with M16s eyed the onlookers with seeming suspicion. Maybe that was part of the mystique, maybe it was PR, maybe it was real, but people still gawked and leaned way over that first line of rope defense.

Each plane was stenciled with the name of the man who flew it. The pilots were there too, ready to answer questions. They looked chiseled, sculpted and trim in gray flight suits. When they started to sign autographs, I knew they were human. They were both younger and older that I expected. Actually I don't know what I expected. Who really knows what kind of pilot flies a secret geometric machine, except probably the best that America can train?

I asked one pilot if the Nighthawk was the best plane he had ever flown. He said he liked the F-15 better. Before my surprise and awe could wear off, there came a collective hush. People all over the tarmac stopped and looked. Even children listened and watched, somehow knowing that the hush was special.

It was the softest hush, with the most power, I had ever heard as the B-2 bomber approached. Silent! It was a thin line out of a distant hazy thinness, rapidly growing bigger as it neared the airfield. Suddenly it was overhead, a thousand feet above. A flyover. No sound. No warning! No wonder they call it *Spirit*. This deltoid wing was ghost-like, an apparition and perhaps, to the uninitiated, something seemingly extraterrestrial.

Once on the ground it was certainly omnipotent in a brief presentation: a mysterious icon shrouded in black composite robes, receiving homage from the excited multitudes and attended to by a stoic, priest-like military. I hadn't seen this kind of adulation since the Pope came to America. People, old and young, pushed and jostled just to get closer to see it. The shoving bordered on rudeness. It was nothing violent, yet catatonically assertive in the need to get close.

The B-2's engines stayed running. The high-pitched engine noise added to the myth and called the throngs to techno-vespers. The plane flexed its ailerons and flaps and blinked its lights at the crowd but stayed aloof and just far enough away from the exuberant fans who wanted to rush and touch her. Military police stood guard. Alert! Weapons ready. Secrets to guard.

The B-2's brief stop on the taxiway was designed to acknowledge and perhaps to placate the blind tithing of the taxpayers. Three billion dollars plus per plane. Maybe more. That was enough for me! The mystery disappears when you add up the cost, but not the appreciation for the human intellect that conceived and created this machine. A masterpiece!

There are probably secret needs and deterrent reasons for this airplane that I don't understand, but can you imagine what that kind of unfathomable money could do to fund a thousand other worthy causes: making a crippled child walk, a blind person see, or even feeding the world's hungry? Such unrealistic dreams!

Enough Pollyanna! I did like that airplane!

ECLIPSE, A SONNET

We knew it to be and then it was there—
The light and the dark playing a game,
Eclipsing the Moon with Earth in the flare,
Crossing the path of the Sun's brightest flame.
The bright slowly slips from light to shadow,
Casting what's left of its bright to below.
With much of the Earth now bathed in a glow,
The Mountains and Lakes sustain their tableaux.
It doesn't last long, but enough to see
The wonder of grace in orbits at dance
That says to the soul, "Be free and then BE,"
Flipping the light while Gaia's in trance.
So often our thoughts eclipse like an Earth,
Keeping our light from a spiritual birth.

SOME THOUGHTS ON THE WORLD'S SOUL

Recently a man said to me, "The world has lost its soul." It may seem like that with so many stories of pain and hate, but the man is wrong!

The recent clarion calls for hurricane aid and the generous response are a case in point. The call for earthquake and tsunami help in Asia echoed through the hearts of the compassionate the world over. By the millions people gave, and give, gifts of time and material. Giving and service are the outward manifestation of the soul of the world.

Overwhelmingly people responded to the collective ache of humankind and came together to validate a friendship of strangers.

No one knows the names of those who receive the gifts. It doesn't matter; names are not important when you know someone is in need. The human face is one in time of need. Millions looked upon that face and responded with abundance.

Despite the shattered peace in parts of this old planet, we have seen the world's soul and it is beautiful.

SOME THOUGHTS ON EXECUTION

If there are no other stays, by this time tomorrow night Michael Ross will be dead, executed in Connecticut.

He murdered, and because of that, he will forfeit his life.

The families and friends of his victims must once again face their sorrow and see if Ross's execution and the witness of it will ease their pain. I suspect there will always be emptiness, a piece of their hearts they cannot mend, and we should do what we can to comfort them.

It's unlikely there will ever be a consensus on the efficacy of the death penalty. There is no way to satisfactorily compile statistics as to whether or not death is a deterrent to murder. The destiny of agreement may only be a perennial debate.

Perhaps the question we should ask ourselves is not whether the person deserved to die—the law decides that—but how do we individually react to it? There are many valid emotions from righteousness to relief. Vengeance, however, is not one of them. It is emotionally consuming and eternally unsatisfying. No wonder a higher authority claimed it a long time ago.

THE SOUL

There is a truth you may not know:
There is no soul within your form.
It's just too big for it to stow
Somewhere within a body norm.

Consider this! All's turned around.
The body's form is in the soul
And gets its life from that surround!
Now, there is a reversal role.

Now think it through a little more.
Uncommon sense from what we think,
That body's form could hold the core
Of Spirit's light without a blink.

So when your path is lighted bright
From more than work or what you say,
It is a beam from soul's spotlight,
An outward ray of love's bouquet.

If energy then follows thought
And manifests from thinking dreams,
No wonder what our acts have wrought
If beams of thought were once blasphemes.

We've looked around and held the sad
Of others' plights just living life,
And wondered, does this mean they're bad,
Resulting in such times of strife?

The answer's no; there's only good
But misdirected from the mind.
It starts creating, as it should,
When thinking is not Source divined.

Thus bring the light within your heart
And know creation is there too
For likes attract right from the start.
A simple truth used by so few.

CITY'S SOUL, 9/11–A NEW YORK SONNET

Old Gotham's sound is a distinctive din
That holds its life above the cobbled cracks
Of past ancient hopes and new youthful sin.
Lives rest in quarried stone and window stacks
Where lonely sighs of want are often heard
In whimpers of weak smiles and hard hurts.
See then dispassion's stance become absurd
For One connects to All and then converts
The sound into a light for bloodless veins.
But soon it calms the raging fear within
And sees the daily stains of processed pains
Dissolve below the stone of annealed skin.
You'll hear the city scream and you'll feel it
Before you know its soul is exquisite.

SOME THOUGHTS ON THE GATES IN CENTRAL PARK

Some like it. Some don't, but it has succeeded in attracting visitors and comment. And like the brilliant beauty of a colorful sunset, it will pass all too quickly.

Seeing the winding and flowing Gates reminds us of our harmonic connection to the creative urge, to nature, to each other and to the infinite beauty of the universe both inner and outer. This singular exhibit by artists Christo and Jeanne-Claude is a visual link between the spirit of a community and its unique perceptions of what is art.

The creations of the great masters, for instance, calm the turmoil of the mind and soothe the worries and pains of daily life, for they transport us to another place and another time through the medium of imagination and appreciation. So does the modern art of the saffron Gates, for they bring color and flow to the drabness of winter gray in a park of play and peace.

Art, in all its forms, cultivates the intellect, personifies the heart and embraces the spirit into a synergy with the sacred. The Gates, through their vibrant color and wind-blown movement, engender a new understanding of creative expression. It's called wonder.

Art, however it is presented, is essential for a civic soul to thrive and to expand. No culture can live without art, and no city should.

PAGEANT OF THE MASTERS

True masters of the pageant
Are ancient artisans
Whose mural art and sculpture
Of life, though still, are held
Anew in shallow breaths
Of living thespians
In silence on a tableau stage
As form and stillness meld.

From canvas, bronze, and jewels
And porcelain figurine,
The objets d'art and paintings
Engender sentient awe
From those who are the spirit
And living unforeseen,
Hidden in the clay and glaze
When artists' hands withdraw.

Everywhere the sculptured light
And music blend as one,
Filling all expecting joy
With brimming flowing grace;
Mindful of collective love,
Beyond comparison
To all creations ever seen,
Held by One's embrace.

Just beyond the even' dark,
'Neath artificial light

Looks of ease are hard sustained
By power from within
Both art and self, when first it was
And conception did excite
The sacred living spark between
The Source and discipline.

The masters are the pageant,
And we appreciative
Of careful authenticity
Held true by grace and form
In recreated portraits,
Precise, comparative,
To the image of the art.
Thus art anew is born.

UNIVERSAL THOUGHT

Would that we could see far beyond the eye
To where the mind oft goes to be alone,
Where mystery blends with thoughts that never die,
And magic melts the ice of what's unknown.
The miracle of mind is what's not seen
Except when artist's hands can clearly show
The universe and time set in between
The silence and the thought—a vast tableau.
What greater gift is there but to create
And greet imagination at its core.
It is in bringing forth that we await
The opening of wonder at the door.
The mind is just the hook to hold the thought
Before we let it go and what it's wrought.

Hard Words

It is the hardest thing I do
To tell my son it's soon he'll die.
But though we know the words are true,
Our hearts are empty from the cry.

The cause is cancer's demon cells,
A curse that's lingered five plus years.
There are no earthly healing bells
To linger with the mournful tears.

We cannot hold him to this plane.
He has a choosing destiny
To pass beyond the cancer drain,
Where growth is spirit's legacy.

Rejoice, my friends, rejoice his life.
We'll miss him one and miss him all.
Though hearts do bleed from dying's knife,
We all must heed the Source's call.

Some Thoughts on Nature

Given the immense devastation throughout Southern Asia, how do we understand the deaths of thousands upon thousands of men, women and children? To say nothing of billions in property losses? It is almost inconceivable.

We seemingly understand that *hate* kills so many every year, but with hate we usually have someone to blame and we focus our energies on protection and retribution and we struggle to keep our actions just short of revenge.

Vengeance has always been claimed by a higher authority.

But now we come to nature. Tidal waves, hurricanes, tornadoes, blizzards, oppressive heat—we have little protection from these random forces and yet we know they occur every year. It's a bit arrogant to blame God and a bit naive to think it won't happen here or to me.

I do know we abuse nature and disrespect its balance, and I hope our science will someday have the knowledge to protect nature and us from each other.

SEASONS' SONNET

As the seasons pass and each time blends in
From the one that departs, there's a graceful
Tranquil moment for the new to begin
Emerging from a place invisible.
This enchanting change is expectancy,
A dawning time, neither a first nor last—
Just new—for seasons are a pregnancy,
A renewing, a birth, a soul recast.
So swaddle the seasons, hold them to see
Summer's bright fall and the white winter's spring.
Cradle the change in a sweet harmony
Of seasons in song and the new they bring.
Seasons and blendings, coming and going,
The blessings of change, ever bestowing.

SOME THOUGHTS ON A STORM

What a glorious time for me! I was outdoors most of the day and saw playful storm clouds tease the mountains with dancing light and shadows as, on and off, passing showers spread a few sprinklings to the valley where I stood in awe.

The distance, as a singular and sentient entity, used the Sun as a Hollywood director would and lit the far-off mountains with a colorful purple brilliance that few see in a lifetime, let along in a single day. The light was a prayer with no words. It was a personal caressing with no touch. It was a symphony with a score of shadows and crescendo's brilliance.

Then I moved to another place of peace, and there, as if it were a package tied, decorated and ready to be unwrapped by all who saw it, was a high-definition opening in a canopy of green to the heightened May blue of sky.

High, very high, and circling was a golden eagle. I do not know whether it was male or female. It did not matter, for the Sun's reflection on its under-wings made it a precious idol, an auric icon of the Great Spirit's manifestation on the Earth, and that was enough for me.

I have seen and felt the same God-presence in the beauty of a rose. I have seen and felt the same spiritual connection in the fragrance of a pine forest after a summer rain and in the drifts of sparkling snow as they pillow white softness upon the Earth. I have seen and felt the same oneness in the tunes of little birds when they sing their songs.

The eagle has now gone and so has the light on the mountains, but not the beauty, not the fragrance, not the aroma, not the sparkle, nor the songs, for they are forever, not only within my heart, but within my words.

I wish you could have been there!

WALL OF STONE

My springtime stroll along the woods and stream
Disclosed a past where others left a sign
Upon the land with dappled lines, a seam,
To mark the place where boundaries intertwine.
I walk along the rocky walls that tie
The grass and woods into a lasting gift.
A granite spirit hums a lullaby
In memory of hard-calloused hands that lift.
Some piled stones are smooth and some edged hard
Yet set in even height and strength throughout.
Who knew the wall would be a lasting guard
To hold the other's space with rocks redoubt?
The wall still has a task this morning fine
Tending now to the honeysuckle vine.

© Charlebois Photography

SOME THOUGHTS ON LISTENING

Listening is difficult for most people. We have some-how erroneously learned that the one who asserts, spouts or comments first is more likely to make a point, win an argument, or impress someone with alleged wit or wisdom.

Accurate and truthful communication requires clarity and simplicity, and it requires listening. It requires stopping to hear with a receptive mind and then processing what was heard. An unfortunate con-dition is that most people only hear what they want to hear, because they don't listen. How many of us, while looking like we are listening, are inwardly thinking of what we are going to say?

Competition in our culture puts a premium on self-expression. What we lack in knowledge we some-times make up for by talking fast, shouting or arguing.

Good listening is a virtue and a courtesy. It helps us to connect to the inner truth of a person. When that happens, serious conversations can go deeper. Arguments over meaningless accusations or questions end, issues are more clearly understood, and verbal conflict is reduced.

Autumn

Despite the frost of autumn's chill,
When all the other leaves are gone,
Some clustered leaves hold to the Oak,
Their summer sheen now brown and still.

What keeps these leaves so tight to limb
As winter breezes quake and shake?
Perhaps the tree is filled with loss
And holds its cloak till colors dim.

For people too it's apropos
To hold and love in fear of loss,
Forgetting nature's truth foretold:
To always have, you must let go.

SOME THOUGHTS ON POETRY

Since today is President John F. Kennedy's birthday, I am reminded of what he said about poetry at the dedication of the Robert Frost Library:

"When power leads man towards arrogance, poetry reminds him of his limitation. When power narrows the areas of man's concern, poetry reminds him of the richness and diversity of his existence. When power corrupts, poetry cleanses. For art establishes the basic human truth which must serve as the touchstone of our judgment."

I would add to that:

Poetry precipitates emotion into words.

Poetry embraces the perceived pain of life and breaks it down into soft images of understanding. Poetry takes the joy of life and transcends it into a sustaining ecstasy of imagination.

Poetry amplifies the tiny specks of grace from the minutiae of things beautiful and allows us to be it, if only for the moment of appreciation.

Poetry clarifies and sometimes condemns. It magnifies the inner magic of feelings and encourages the soul to rejoice in the shared awareness of another's insight and makes it our own.

Poetry laughs and cries and brings the sensual into an undulating body of words. It holds, sometimes forever, an emotion long past, a desire forgotten, a wish remembered or a splendor vanished in the illusion of time.

Poetry is a link to the Divine within each of us and to the demons of our imagination. It allows introspection without pity, and effacement without fear of obscurity.

Poetry is intellect and spirit wedded in the sacredness of creation. I believe it is agape love at the purest verbal level.

SPRING

New growth appears to soothe the weary eye
When March winds leave and April's sun arrives.
It warms the looming might within the earth
And green becomes the bright of life's rebirth.

We said good-bye to colors soft with scent
Just months ago when summer's light was spent.
We welcomed then the cold of winter's rite
And shivered at the crystal dunes of white.

But once again we're back to birth anew
As seeds begin to stretch for their debut.
When spring arrives, the earth renews her smile,
And soon we'll see her flowered grace beguile.

Some Thoughts on the Pursuit of Elegance

There is much discussion about talk shows these days. The common complaint is content: public promiscuity, gratuitous attack, abusive relationships, verbal hate, interruption and yelling; it goes on and on.

No one talks of elegance. No one talks of grace. No one talks of beauty, and yet these qualities are inherent in our nature. We all were born with the ability to appreciate, to have creative dignity in our thoughts and expectations and to see the profound interconnectedness of all things.

Where are the talk shows that feature the efficacy of gentleness, kindness, positive acts of service, miracles, selfless and unconditional love, courage, spirit and things artistic, as expressed through form and language? Gentility is a facet of everyday life worthy of telling about, and teaching by the being of it. It has a value far beyond the degenerating voyeurism into other people's pain and problems solely for the purpose of ratings.

The sad truth is not that the talk shows exploit the sordid stories and the banal characteristics of life, but that there is no offering of an elegant alternative. We deserve better; we can demand better.

OAK SONNET

Old rusted Oaks hold firm their foliage
While other trees have shed to silhouette!
Are leafy hoards, now dead, a sacrilege?
Or does the Oak hold leaves as amulet?
Soon winter's wind unlocks, and leaves release
But still we'll not know why this is the way,
For Oaks have always had a staying peace
That reason cannot change or cast away.
The Druids saw their Oaks as sacred trees
And to them prayed for guidance and support,
But that meant not they must release their leaves
To be, in fall, the way most trees abort.
The mighty Oaks and man are much the same:
When ready we release what we became.

Some Thoughts on Collective Consciousness

I Am One with All That Is in a singular breath of NOW and in the illusionary moment of time. When the "I" sees the vastness within the One, it knows the whole is interconnected in a cosmic refrain of personal joy and collective consciousness. The "I" is then "Am-ed" in a spiritual experience of profound realization that growth is not singular but the shared harmony of awareness.

From the instantaneous moment of creation, we have each asked "Who am I?" The question is eternal, and the answer is simple in truth and complex in understanding. We are the individuation of the indivisible. We are God! We were created from the Source for God to experience Himself/Herself through us, as us. We each are the quantum experience of the Divine in the eternal omnipresent enfoldment of love. Unfortunately we have forgotten this truth through the gracious gift of choice, but life is the ongoing opportunity to choose, at any time, to consciously remember our divinity. When we do, WONDER is the result.

There is, however, a responsibility when the realization of Oneness becomes the precipitate of awareness. When you know that each and every life form is connected by invisible strands of sacred energy, and between stones and saints the only difference of BEING is awareness, then each and every choice must be considered in reference and relevance to the gestalt and not to an appeasement to the ego in the desire of momentary want.

To "Am" our own "I" is why we choose life. It's why we come into this density and into this form. We are spirit beings blessed in the co-creation and manifestation of physical matter via choice. Matter has always followed thought!

In the intellectual process of attempted understanding of "Who I Am," there is a collective consciousness of shared experience, even though spiritually there is only one consciousness. Sharing our experience and identity in order to objectify our thoughts into a collective consciousness is a powerful step toward the Oneness with All That Is. We have always been and always will be ONE; we just have to remember that we are.

It starts by knowing and accepting that we are divine. We are the magnificent physical manifestation of Spirit. We cannot not be part of what created us. We are love. We cannot *not* be something we are. We can only forget until we remember, and when we do, it will be a knowing that when you know you know—you know!

When finally we choose to be the evidence of what it is we are, the collective becomes ONE and consciousness is experienced through the interconnected vision of unconditional love.

Tonight, today, yesterday and now there is an on-going invitation for all of us to be courageous—to be true to ourselves.

It is an invitation to share a mythical journey by seeing our own passage through the sharing of stories, conversations, service and questions. We are all prodigal children, who, as adults, may return to the comfort of innocence by questioning the choices that have brought each of us to this moment in life.

Every journey, in order to ultimately embrace the truth of who we are and to shed the illusions of life and time, must slay the daily dragons in the caves of self-creation. But dragons cannot be slain with the social weapons of today: cell phones, briefcases, contracts, jobs or even atavistic beliefs embedded in human history. Illusionary dragons are slain by peeling away the material attachments of stuff and connecting once again to the Source, to the divinity within each of us as us.

Today and tonight and even tomorrow as we pass through each other's lives and thoughts, we each are a reminder to the other that we can find our authentic selves only by going within to the still point of the divine, and then as we return to the daily demands of life, to a living sometimes expressed in suits and dresses, in events and duty, in noise and fear, we take with us the knowing that only through unconditional love and public and private appreciation of things beautiful can we find the solace of the Source.

We might choose to remember, when we are mired in the density of frustration and the tears of emotion, that we are more than we seem. We are the culmination of genetic sediment upon which is built the self via experience and personal memory.

I believe that each of us receives guidance and blessings from spirits who live forever in the universal light of ancestry and in the angelic realms of inspirational belief and counsel.

These guides, if you will, collectively ask that we remember the divine rhythm, remember it through our chants and prayers, remember it through the observed beauty and profound grace of this planet, and they ask us to dance the life dance that links us to the Source, to the All That Is, to the beneficence of so many names. They ask that we forget old hates, prejudices, fears and retributions we may have been taught, for they are the absolute illusions that keep the dragons alive.